PHOTOGRAPHS & POEMS

PHOTOGRAPHS & POEMS

Salvatore Mancini

INCORPORATED

·ASPEN. COLORADO·

Library of Congress Number 73-88289
I.S.B.N. 0-914120-00-X Softbound

Dedication

What is the difference between Self-
realization and God-realization?
My belief is that they are one
and the same. This book is dedicated
to that concept.

Introduction

As assuredly as no bird
          ever slurred his words,
the painter will at times paint
as though placing pieces of flesh
            onto his canvas.
The poet at times writes
with his penis as well as his hands.
The writer closes his eyes and reads
the book he is about to write.
The sculptor believes that he is releasing
the life form imprisoned within.
The photographer learns to treat
the photographic emulsion as a sheet of skin;
layers of dormant life which he gives birth to.
The artist in expressing
the dimensions of his life,
becomes as sensitive and truthful
as a dog with his tail.
Assuredly . . . .
as waves are not borders on the sea.

Such a poor man i am.
I awoke to the lifting sounds
      of a springbirdsong,
      of winds wooshing by, sweeping
their slumberence over the tree field me.
My hair tumbles into clumps
        of matted sea grass.
Thousands of muffled fingers titillate
my ear drums and mind chimes.
From my toasty bed
i can see the dozing sun rise,
      becoming momentarily frozen
      onto my frosted window,
a soggy thaw
hovering over a crystallized landscape,
interlaced with soft shadowy branches
and rolling hills of friable iceflakes.
But i wasn't inspired.   What is wrong with me?

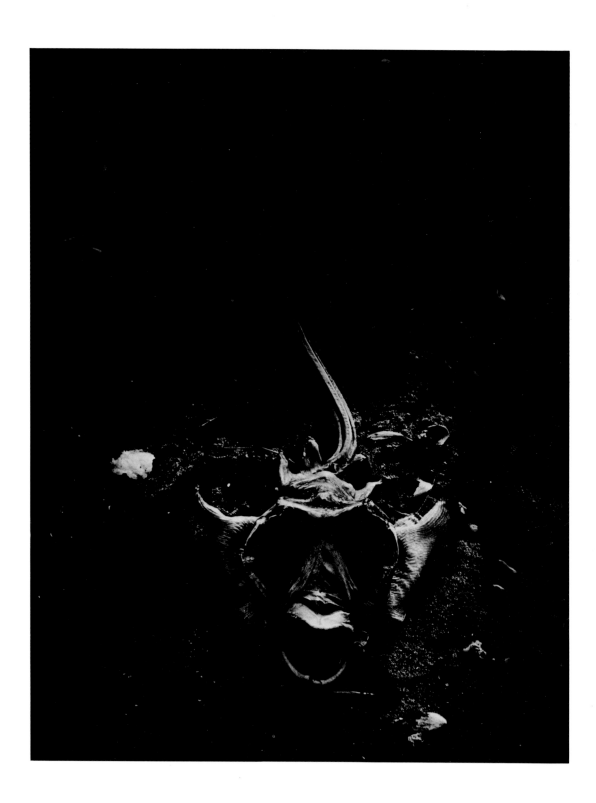

A leaf propelled
by the winds
has no power
of its own.
A man driven by
an inspiration
is never alone.

I walk out
        into the early morning still pond
to gather my thoughts
        among this eluding dewy world.
My skin is made soft
        by the osmosiating mist.
Quietly my thoughts rise
        beyond the eyes and i . . . then . .
filling my cupped hands
        with assorted people pebbles,
i scattered them far into the no sound pond.
Each creates and regenerates a whirl; a world
                                within a whirl
                                within a world.
There is nothing more i can say of this life.

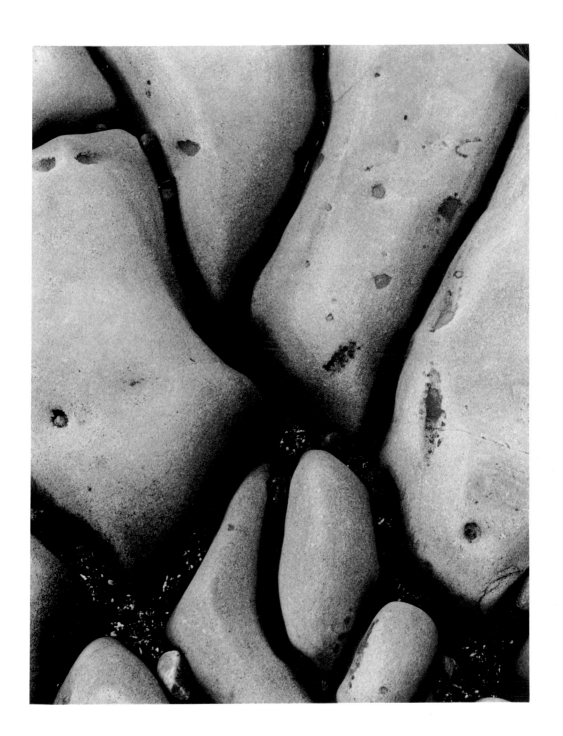

Sun Eyes
Sun Rise
Sun Skies
Sun I

You ask:
    "What is it about you
      that i love so much?"
I reply:
    "You."
You say:
    "Your eyes, they are so beautiful."
I answer:
    "Look at what they see."
You ask:
    "Am i wrong to believe
      that it is love which binds us?"
I reply:
    "Yes . . . for love gives freedom."

Waiting for you . . . . . .
        that is the depth of my loneliness.
The sun has faded my body
from the countless exiled days
at my sleepless window.
               My hoping,
a devoted puppy nibbling at my heels.

Who are you . . . . . .
that you can make me lonelier than a god?
My matted pillow lies sunken,
entombed with my smudged face.
A misanthropic sleepwalker
trudging through a damp purgatory.

You saw it too . . . . didn't you!?
                    DIDN'T YOU!?
With the evening star
beginning to shimmer,
i stood beneath
the paling moon,
a snowball of wrinkled skin
winging across the gloom,
                blighted by my own aloneness.
But bold, SO BOLD.
Didn't i look Godlike . . . .
    didn't i, didn't i!?
    Please say i did, i did!
    . . . . Me,
this bloated facade
of ecclesiatic delights
shivering in my
naked bones
as all cadavers
of becauses do,
trying to warm myself
by the light of the stars.

Why does a laughing
man close his eyes ?
With nothing to do
i stopped to watch
a butterfly glide
effortlessly through the breeze.
Queen Ann's lace
and groves of clover;
how jealous i've
become of you.
Your petals hold the sky
in their pools of dew.
Grasshoppers vacation
in your shade.
Butterflies know you by name
and ever since the first
celestial burst
proclaimed i throughout.
A cellular gesture
grew with the question why;
i've been searching
        for a home.

Energy, Energy, Energy . . . .
surges of creative impulses, untamed flames,
fragmenting known into mysterious,
            swelling my being;
a bubble about to burst into shreds
            of emancipated spirits,
            fits of worldly amazements,
            reservoirs of gushing anticipations.
And in the ephemeral afterglow,
a long list of heroic promises to myself,
   (all the selves who claimed to be me,)
to work, to deeds, to accomplishments.
            Then with the first doubt
            the piranhas emerge.
My ego bloats itself on the conceit of its
omnipotent connection.
      (Oh, didn't you know? All the Prophets,
        Indian Chiefs and Sun Kings,
        have these experiences.)
My fears begin to feast,
insecurities, inertia, boredom . . . .
                        munch, munch, crunch.
My sexual appetite wallows in its own consumption.
Every distraction
            snatches a handful in passing.
What energy is left,
            dribbles out of my mouth,
                  in exhausted words.

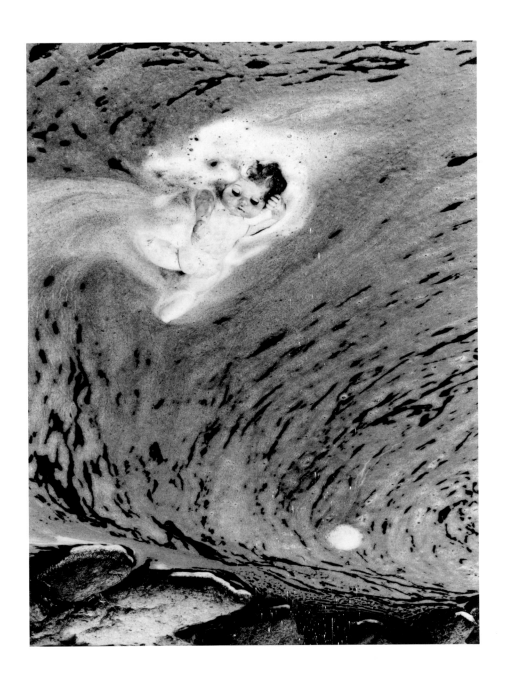

Do not be afraid
if your body tosses suddenly
from a motionless sleep.
It is only my heart
reaching out for you.